# MEDEA OF EURIPIDES.

*LITERALLY TRANSLATED INTO*

*ENGLISH VERSE*

BY

AUGUSTA WEBSTER.

London and Cambridge:
MACMILLAN AND CO.
1868

[*All Rights reserved.*]

Augusta Webster

**The Medea of Euripides**

ISBN/EAN: 9783337189099

Printed in Europe, USA, Canada, Australia, Japan

Cover: Foto ©ninafisch / pixelio.de

More available books at **www.hansebooks.com**

The text upon which this translation is based is that of Paley (London, 1857). A list of the passages in which different readings have been taken will be found at the end.

The numbers within brackets refer to the corresponding lines in Paley.

# DRAMATIS PERSONÆ.

Nurse.
Attendant on Medea's Children.
Medea.
Chorus of Corinthian Women.
Creon.
Jason.
Ægeus.
Messenger.
Medea's Children.

# MEDEA.

### Nurse.

OULD the ship Argo ne'er had fetched her flight
Twixt the dark Symplegades to Colchian land,
And the cleft pine in Pelion's woods ne'er fallen,
Nor caused the chieftains' hands to row, who went
To seek the golden fleece for Pelias.  5 (5)
For neither then Medea, mistress mine,
Had sailed to the Iolchian country's towers,
By love for Jason stricken at the heart;
Nor, having wrought upon the damsels, race
Of Pelias, to slay their sire, had dwelt  10 (9)
With husband and with sons in Corinth here,
So pleasuring in sooth the citizens

Of the country she has come to, by that flight,
Herself to Jason in all things conformed—
In which the better part of safety lies      15 (14)
That the woman should not differ from the man.
Now all's ajar and dearest love is sick :
For, his children and my mistress both betrayed,
Jason in royal spousals beds him, wed
To Creon's daughter, liege lord of this land. 20 (19)
But Medea, the forlorn, dishonoured cries
Upon his oaths, appeals to that chief troth
Of plighting hands, and calls the gods to mark
With what requital she from Jason meets.
Refusing food, her body anguish-prone,      25 (24)
Floating the hours from her in tears, she lies
Since first she knew her by her husband wronged ;
And will not raise her eyes, nor from the ground
Lift up her face.  As a rock might or sea-wave,
Does she hear those who love her counselling her,
Save when, averting her so pallid neck,     31 (30)
For her dear father she bemoans herself,
Her land and home deserted when she fled
With the man who does her this dishonour now.
She, hapless, sees now in her misery        35 (34)

What 'twere, not to have lost one's fatherland.
She loathes her sons, nor now joys seeing them.
Aye, but I dread her lest she plot some burst:
For she's high-stomached, nor will tamely bear
Wrongs put on her; I know her and I doubt her
Lest she slay those royal ones, yea and with them
The bridegroom, and go on to worser ills:
For she's unbending: not with ease, forsooth,
Will any sworn her foe chant victory.
But I perceive her boys, their races ceased, 45 (46)
Coming, unmindful of their mother's griefs;
—For the young heart cares not to sorrow long.

### ATTENDANT.

Thou good old chattel of my lady's home,
Why, dawdling solitary at the gates,
Dost stand and croon of troubles to thyself? 50 (51)
Why has Medea willed thee leave her thus?

### . NURSE.

Reverend attendant upon Jason's sons,
The masters' luck fallen wrong to worthy servants
Is their calamity and racks their hearts:
And I have reached to such a pitch of pain 55 (56)

That yearning came on me to pass out here
And cry to earth and heaven my lady's woes.

### ATTENDANT.

And she, sad woman, slacks not yet her moans?

### NURSE.

Hear him! Grief's at the start, not near half-way.

### ATTENDANT.

Oh fool—were't fit to speak thus of our lords—
How all unconscious of the newer ills!  61 (62)

### NURSE.

And what are they, old man? Grudge not to tell.

### ATTENDANT.

Nought. I am vexed for what's already said.

### NURSE.

By thy beard, hide nothing from thy fellow slave:
For I'll keep silence, if need be, on all.  65 (66)

### ATTENDANT.

I heard one say, I seeming not to hear,
As I came near the draught-boards where the old men

11

Around Pirene's sacred water sit,
That, with their mother, from the soil of Corinth,
The realm's lord, Creon, exiles presently     70 (71)
The boys.  In sooth thus runs the tale: if true
I know not.  But I pray it be not thus.

### NURSE.

What, and will Jason see his sons so used,
Even though he be in quarrel with their mother?

### ATTENDANT.

New ties stand foremost to the old.  Henceforth
Towards this home he has no kindliness.    76 (77)

### NURSE.

We are undone then if to the first ill,
Ere yet it be drained dry, we add a new.

### ATTENDANT.

But thou, since for our lady to hear this
'Tis no fit time, peace, and hush up the news.

### NURSE.

Oh children, hear ye what your father is?    81 (82)
I pray—no harm on him, he is my master;
But sure he is proved an ill friend to his kin.

ATTENDANT.

What man is other?—Dost thou learn but now
That each before his neighbour loves himself— (86)
Some fairly, but some with the greed of gain?
As when, belike, for new espousals' sake
This father is no father to his sons.

NURSE.

Go in the house boys: all will yet be well. 89 (89)
Thou, to the utmost, keep them by themselves,
Nor bring them near their sorrow-frenzied mother.
For late I saw her with the roused bull's glare
View them as though she'd at them. And I trow
That she'll not bate her wrath till it have swooped
On some prey. Be it foe then and not friend!

MEDEA (*heard speaking within*).
Woe's me!
Forlorn that I am, borne down with despair! 96 (96)
Woe worth the while! If I might but die!

NURSE.

There, 'tis as I said, your mother, dear boys,
Is lashing her will, is lashing her wrath:

Hurry on faster then into the house;  100 (100)
Approach ye not near her within her sight;
Go not to greet her; rather keep watch and ward
Against her wild mood and the virulent bent
 Of her ruthless mind.
Go, go, pass within, as you quickliest can.  105 (105)
It is plain to see that the cloud of grief,
Waxing and waxing since first it rose,
Will kindle ere long in stronger wrath.
And what will her passionate conquerless soul
 Stung by such wrongs compass then?  110 (110)

  MEDEA (*still speaking within*).
 Ah me! ah me!
I have endured, sad woman, endured
A burden for great laments. Cursed sons
Of a loathed mother die, ye and your sire,
 And let all our house wane away!

  NURSE.
Woe worth the while! Sad woman, ah me!  115 (115)
But why are the boys made part in the crime
Of their father? Why turn on them? Alas,
Boys, how I anguish lest you come to harm.

Dread are the humours of princes : as wont
To be ruled in few things and in many to lord,
It is hard to them to turn from their wrath.
(But to lead one's life in the level ways
Is best) Be it mine then to pass to old age
If no way high placed yet calmly secure.   124 (124)
\ For there's vantage just in speaking the name
Of the golden mean : \and to have it and hold
Is past all best for man. (But too high-pitched luck
Stands no mortal in stead at the time of need;)
Nay, more, when the god is stirred to his wrath,
    Dowers greater curse on the house. / 130 (130)

*End of Prologue.*

## CHORUS.
*Parode*

I heard the voice, nay heard the shriek
    Of the hapless Colchian dame.
Is she not calmed? Old matron, speak—
    For through the double portals came
        A voice of wail and woe.   135 (135)
Nor, women, is it mine to share
Joy at this house's now despair,
    My friend from long ago.

### NURSE.
*Episode.*
Here's no more a home, home-things are all fled ;
For he is kept hence by a royal couch,  140 (140)
While in her chamber my lady alone
Weeps away life, and no way is calmed
  At heart by the words of her friends.

### MEDEA (*still speaking within*).
Woe! woe!
Oh lightning from heaven dart through my head!
For what is my gain to live any more?  145 (145)
Alas! alas! Might I cease in death,
  Escaping from hated life!

### CHORUS.
*Stasimon*
#### STROPHE.
Oh Zeus dost thou perceive, and Earth, and Light,
What wail plains out the desolate young wife?
And why should love-pangs for thy wedded right,
Speed thee, poor fool, to end in death the strife?
      Nay, pray not so :
And if thine husband worship a new bride
Chafe not thyself—Zeus will judge on thy side—
Nor mourn thy spouse with too exceeding woe.  155 (159)

MEDEA (*still speaking within*).
Oh thou great Themis, and Sovereign Artemis,
Do you see what I bear, I who had bound
By terrible oaths my accursed spouse—
Whom with his bride may I one day behold
Crushed into atoms, they and their halls,  160 (164)
They who have dared the first wrong and on me?
Oh father! oh country! whom I forsook
Traitorous, slaying my brother first.

NURSE.
Do ye hear how she speaks and makes her cry
To Themis invoked in the vow, and to Zeus,  165 (169)
Since he is deemed lord over mortal oaths?
It may not be that my lady shall stay
　　Her rage with a little thing.


CHORUS.

ANTISTROPHE.
Oh would she coming in our sight attend
That oracle of words we spake, if aught  170 (175)
May move her gloom and wrath. But never friend

Lack zeal of mine. Then go, let her be brought
    Hither outside the gate ;
And bid her know me friend. But speed thee well,
Lest on those there with her some mischief fell 175 (184)
She wreak: so has her passion swelled of late.

NURSE.

I will do as ye bid, but there's fear lest I fail
    My lady to win.
Yet I will give you my pains in free boon,
Although with the gaze of a lioness    180 (187)
With newborn cubs does she glare at her slaves,
If any approach her proffering speech.
And sure ye would not err if ye said
The men of old times were rude and nought wise,
Who fashioned for revels and wassails and feasts
Songs that make life by listening delight,    186 (194)
While no mortal has yet devised to lull
By music and chants many-toned the loathed pangs
When death and strange fates tread down homes.
And yet to calm these with the measured strain 190 (199)
Were in sooth a gain unto men: but why
Raise the vain sound where the feast is glad?

2

For the feast with its present fullness alone
   Is itself a delight for men.

#### CHORUS.

    I heard a voice of sighs       195 (204)
    And groaning long laments,
    Where she, with shrilly cries,
    Her bitter anguish vents
Against the traitor her false lord,
And, bowed with wrong, she makes her prayer 200 (207)
To Themis, child of Zeus, whose care
    Is the plighted word—
    Themis, she
Who hither to our Hellas brought her,
Crossing o'er the night-dusk water,     205 (211)
The salt straits of the unending sea.

#### MEDEA.

Women of Corinth, I come from the house
Lest ye should blame me. I know many men
Are counted arrogant, some that they keep from sight,
Some that they are in public, and to those   210 (216)
Who walk in calm comes ill repute of sloth.

For justice dwells not in the eyes of mortals,
Theirs who, before they inly know a man,
Look and straight loathe him, nothing wronged by him.
More, it behoves an alien specially          215 (222)
To mould himself unto the city's wont:
Nor can I praise a fractious citizen
Waxed wanton to his folk through ignorance.
But my soul by this all unlooked for weird
Fallen upon me is crushed utterly.           220 (225)
I am undone, and turned from joy of life,
My friends, I am in very need to die.
For he in whom was all to me, my husband,
Ye know it well, has proved of men most base.
Aye, of all living and of reasoning things   225 (230)
Are woman the most miserable race:
Who first needs buy a husband at great price,
To take him then for owner of our lives:
For this ill is more keen than common ills.
And of essays most perilous is this,         230 (235)
Whether one good or evil do we take.
For evil-famed to women is divorce,
Nor can one spurn a husband. She so brought
Beneath new rule and wont had surely need

To be a prophetess, unless at home        235 (239)
She learned the likeliest prospect with her spouse.
And if, we having aptly searched out this,
A husband house with us not savagely
Drawing in the yoke, ours is an envied life;
But if not, most to be desired is death.    240 (243)
And if a man grow sick to herd indoors,
He, going forth, stays his heart's weariness,
Turning him to some friend or natural peer;
But we perforce to one sole being look.    244 (24⁷)
But, say they, we, while they fight with the spear,
Lead in our homes a life undangerous:
Judging amiss; for I would liefer thrice
Bear brunt of arms than once bring forth a child.
Ah well! the like words fit not thee and me:
For thee there is a country, and for thee    250 (253)
A father's home, for thee are life's delights
And the familiar intercourse of friends;
But I, alone, calling no city mine,
Am outraged by a spouse, I led a prey
From a far land, who have no mother more,    255 (257)
Nor brother, nor a kinsman of my blood,
Where to seek harbour in this evil day.

Therefore this much I fain would gain of you,
That, if I find a way and a device  259 (260)
To recompense my husband for these wrongs,
And her he wed and him who gave his daughter,
Ye will keep counsel. For in other things
Is a woman full of fears and most ill-fit
For battles and to look upon the sword;
But come there treason to her bridal bed  265 (265)
There is no other mind more thirsts for blood.

CHORUS.

This will I do. For righteously wilt thou
Avenge thyself upon thy spouse, Medea:
Nor marvel I that thou dost mourn thy fate.
But I see Creon, sovereign of this land,  270 (269)
Approach, a messenger of new resolves.

CREON. *Exile of Medea*
Thee, sullen-browed and chafing at thy spouse,
Medea, I command that from this realm
Thou go an exile, taking thy two sons.
And linger not, for mine is the decree,  275 (274)
Nor will I enter in my house again
Till I have driven thee past this land's last bounds.

#### MEDEA.

Alas! I hapless perish utterly!
For now my enemies crowd on all sail,
And there is no near haven from despair. 280 (279
But yet, though bowed with wrongs, will I dare speak:
Why dost thou drive me from thy country, Creon?

#### CREON.

I fear thee—it boots not to cloke my thoughts—
Lest thou shouldst work my child some mortal ill.
And many things make jointly to this dread. 285 (284)
Thou art much wise, and subtle in dread lores,
And thou art wroth, lorn of thy husband's bed;
Nay, I hear, threatst, so word came, some dire deed
On bridegroom and on bride and him who gave her.
Therefore I keep guard ere I suffer this. 290 (289)
Aye lady, better win thy present hate
Than, softened by thee, later mourn it long.

#### MEDEA.

Ah me! Ah me!
Not now first, Creon, but a many times
Hath this fame stricken me and wrought me ill.
But never fits it one born prudent-souled 295 (295)

To have his children reared surpassing wise;
For, added to their blame of lavished time,
They win cross envy from their citizens.
For, offering a new wisdom unto fools,
Thou shalt be held a dullard not a sage: 300 (300)
And, if deemed more than those who make a show
Of varied subtleties, then shalt thou seem
A mischief in the city. Yea, myself
I share this fortune, for, being wise, I am
To some a mark for envy, and to some 305 (304)
Abhorrent. Yet I am not very wise.
But thou then fearest me lest thou feel some blow:
Things are not so with me—dread us not, Creon—
That I should do offence to kingly men.
For thou, how hast thou wronged me? Thou hast
 given 310 (309)
Thy girl what way thy mind led. But my husband
I hate. Yet thou, I think, in this didst well.
And now, in sooth, I grudge thee not thy luck:
Make marriages, be prosperous. But this land
Leave me, a home to dwell in: for, though wronged,
I will keep silence, vanquished by my lords. 316 (315)

CREON.

Thou dost speak soft to hear; yet in my mind
Is fear lest thou be planning some foul deed,
And so much less I trust thee than before.
For a woman passionate, yea and a man,   320 (319)
Is easier warded than a silent plotter.
But go forth at the quickest, speak no word;
Since this is fixed, nor hast thou shift by which
Thou shalt stay with us, being my enemy.

MEDEA.

Nay by thy knees, by thy new-wedded child! 325 (324)

CREON.

Thou dost lose words. For thou shalt nought prevail.

MEDEA.

But wilt thou exile me, nor heed my prayers?

CREON.

Since thee I love not more than mine own house.

MEDEA.

My country, how I now remember thee!

CREON.

And next my children is my city dear.   330 (329)

MEDEA.

Ah me! How great an ill to man is love!

CREON.

That is, I doubt, as fortune waits on it.

MEDEA.

Zeus, be it not hid from thee who caused these ills!

CREON.

Hence, thou weak fool, and free me from these troubles.

MEDEA.

I am the troubled, with full store of troubles.   335 (334)

CREON.

Ere long my guards shall thrust thee out by force.

MEDEA.

Nay, nay, not thus. Oh but I pray thee, Creon.

CREON.

Thou wilt cause violence, woman, as I see.

### MEDEA.

We will go forth. I pleaded not of that.

### CREON.

Why dost thou strive then, nor wilt leave this realm? 340 (33

### MEDEA.

Let me remain this one day and revolve
Some plan to fly, some refuge for my boys,
Since the father cares not for his sons to fend.
But pity them: thou also art a father,
And surely dost know natural tenderness.  345 (345)
For me, I care not if we must go forth,
But I weep them now schooled to adversity.

### CREON.

My mind by nature is nought tyrannous,
And oft by pity have I harmed myself:
And now I see, oh woman, that I err:  350 (350)
Yet shalt thou gain this. Yet I do forwarn thee,
If the next coming day's torch of the heavens
Shall see thee and thy boys in this realm's bounds,

Thou diest.  The word that shall not swerve is
   spoken.
But now if stay thou must, stay this one day; 355 (355)
Not so thou'lt compass any deed I dread.
                       (*Exit Creon*).

CHORUS.

   Ah woman forlorn!
Alas for thee worn with thy miseries!
Where now wilt thou turn? with what sheltering host,
What country, what home, a haven for thee 360 (360)
   From woes wilt thou find?
Since the god, Medea, hath guided thy way
   Mid an issueless wave of woes.

MEDEA.

On all sides woes are heaped: who shall deny it?
But it is not yet thus: believe it not.    365 (365)
Still waits there danger for the wedded pair,
And for the marriage-kinsfolk no light pangs.
For thinkest thou that ever I would thus
Have fawned on him wer't not to earn my vantage
And with a plot—no, not so much as spoken, 370 (370)
Not touched him with my hands.  So he has reached

To such a folly that, when it was his
Driving me from his land to thwart my schemes,
He yields me that I stay here yet this day,
In which three of my foes I'll do to death, 375 (374)
The father, and the girl, and him *my* husband.
But, having many ways of death for them,
I know not, friends, which first to take in hand.
Whether shall I set fire to the bridal home,
Or, stealing silent to the nuptial bed, 380 (380)
Pash down my whetted dagger to the heart?
But there's one thing against me. Were I caught
Entering the house and working to mine ends,
Then would my death make laughter for my foes.
Better the easier way, and most akin 385 (384)
To my birthright skill, to take them off by drugs.
    So be it then.
They dead, what city shall receive me in?
What host will, offering me a land of refuge
And home assured, rescue my life? There's none.
Why then, still waiting for a little while 390 (388)
If any tower of safety show for us,
Silent and subtle I'll to this work of death.
But, if a fate resistless drives me forth,

Snatching the sword though 'twere to doom my death,
I'll slay them—yea to the very utmost dare.  395 (393)
For never, by my queen whom I revere
Beyond all else and chose unto my aid,
By Hecate who dwells on my hearth's shrine,
Shall any wring my heart and still be glad.
Aye, sad to them and bitter will I make  400 (398)
The wedding-tide, bitter the plighted bond
And my departing from this land. Go to,
Pondering and planning; spare no skill, Medea:
On to the deed, now is thy bravery tried.
Dost see thy hap? It fits not thou yield mirth  405 (403)
To the race of Sisyphus, Jason's new folk,
Thou born of a great sire, come of the Sun:
And thou art skilled. We women too art born
Most profitless indeed to noble works,
But cunningest devisers of all harms.  410 (408)

### CHORUS.

#### Strophe I.

The hallowed rivers backward stream
Against their founts : right crooks awry

With all things else: man's every scheme
    Is treachery.
Even with gods faith finds no place.     415 (413)
But fame turns too: our life shall have renown:
Honour shall come to woman's race,
And envious fame no more weigh women down.

### CHORUS.

#### Antistrophe I.

No more the staled songs shall be heard
Of muses hymning *our* deceit;     420 (421)
For Phœbus not on us conferred
    The lyre heaven-sweet
Lest we a counter strain should sing
Against the race of men: but ages old
Have in their keeping many a thing     425 (428)
Not of us only but of men to unfold.

### CHORUS.

#### Strophe II.

And thou, grown mad at heart, didst come,
Sailed hither from thy father's home,

Past the twin rocks of the sea,
And dwell'st upon an alien coast.   430 (436)
And now, sad woman, thou hast lost
The shelter that a wife's should be,
Thou widowed as thou art and sent
Dishonoured into banishment.


CHORUS.

### Antistrophe II.

The sanctity of oaths is o'er:   435 (439)
Shame in great Hellas dwells no more,
　　But is vanished into air.
Nor is there father's home for thee,
Forlorn one, where there yet might be
A harbour from thy storm of care:   440 (442)
And in thy house a dearer bride
Now queens it at thy husband's side.


### Jason.

Not the first time now, but often, have I seen
Fierce rage is an irremediable ill.

For thou, to whom remained this land and
    home, 445 (447)
Hadst thou borne meekly thy superiors' will,
Art by thy wild words driven from this realm.
And, for my part, no matter; never cease
From saying Jason is the worst of men:
But, for thy railing at the royal house, 450 (452)
Count it thy gain by exile to be punished.
For me I still was forward to appease
The princes' wrath, and would have had thee stay.
But thou, thou wouldest not leave thy folly, still
Railed at the royal house, and now indeed 455 (457)
Art driven from the realm. And yet I come,
Never weary for my friends, to care for thee,
That not in penury nor any want
Thou go forth with our children. Many hardships
Do wait on exile, and, though thou dost hate
    me, 460 (462)
I am not able to desire thy harm.

### MEDEA.

Oh wholly base—this shall my tongue declare,
The greatest shame to thine unmanliness—

## 33

Thou comest to us, comest, our worst foe.
This is no courage, this no noble strength, 465 (469)
To front it out with friends whom thou hast wronged.
Rather it is man's loathsomest distemper,
Rank shamelessness. But thou dost well to come;
For I, reviling thee, will soothe my heart,
And thou wilt be stung hearing. Yea, and first 470 (474)
I from the first beginning will begin.
I saved thee, as each Hellene knows who sailed
In the ship Argo with thee, thee sent forth
To tame unto the yoke the fire-breathed bulls
And sow the furrow to the deadly strife: 475 (479)
And the dragon who, coiled round the golden fleece,
Fenced it with snaky knots and never slept,
I slew, who stood to thee thy beacon light:
And, traitress to my father and my home,
I, not so wise as loving, came with thee 480 (485)
To Peliot Iolchos: and by death
Of all kind bitterest, by his children's hands,
Pelias I slew and freed thee from all fear.
And, so much owing me, thou, oh worst villain,
Betrayest me and, father of my sons, 485 (490)

Hast a new wedding-bed. Sooth, hadst thou been
Yet childless thy desires had had excuse.
But the faith of oaths is gone, nor can I learn
If thou dost deem the gods no longer rule,
Or that new laws are now decreed for men,   490 (494)
Since thou dost own thyself perjured to me.
Alas this right hand thou didst often clasp!
These knees thou didst entreat by! To vain end
Was I polluted by this bad man's touch;
And all my hopes have ended in deceit.   495 (498)
Come now, I'll reason with thee as a friend—
Yet what way dreaming to get good of thee?
But still—for questioned thou wilt show more base—
Where shall I turn me? To my father's house
Which, with my country, I forsook for thee?   500 (503)
To Pelias' unhappy daughters? Sooth,
Kindly unto their house they'd welcome me
Who slew their father. For this is my case;
With my friends of home I have become at war,
And them whom it ill fitted me to wrong,   505 (507)
For thy sake I have made mine enemies.
And, truly, thou dost guerdon me with bliss
Envied by many a wife in Hellas, sure.

And truly a most perfect loyal spouse
Have I, poor wretch, if banished I go forth,  510 (512)
Barren of friends, alone with my lone children.
Rare fame for the new bridegroom that his sons
And she who saved him beggars roam about.
Oh Zeus why hast thou given mankind sure test
To know the spurious gold, while upon men  515 (517)
Is no mark born whereby to tell a knave?

CHORUS.

Terrible is that anger, and to assuage
Most difficult, when friends with friends join battle.

JASON.

It seems I'd needs be not unapt at words,
But like a skilful pilot sheer away,  520 (524)
Woman, from the jangling of thy wordy tongue.
But since thou dost so much exalt thy service,
I take it Cypris was, of gods and men,
Alone the guardian of my enterprise.
Why yes, thou hast a very crafty wit,  525 (529)
But 'twere invidious to go through the tale
How Eros, with his swift escapeless darts,

Forced it upon thee to preserve my life.
But not too nicely will I count our scores:
For how far thou didst help me 'twas not ill. 530 (533)
But in all truth thou hast for saving me
Gained far beyond thy giving: as I'll show.
First then, instead of thy barbarian land,
Thou dwellst in Hellas, and knowst justice now,
And the help of laws not measured by mere
    force: 535 (538)
And more, now all the Hellenes know thee wise,
And thou hast glory. But, hadst thou still dwelt
In those outmost shores, there were no word of thee.
And be it not mine to heap my house with gold,
Nor to sing sweeter strains than Orpheus, 540 (543)
If such my fortune make me not renowned.
So much then of thy troubles for my sake
I speak: since thou hast made this war of words.
But what thou twitst me with, my royal marriage,
In this I'll show thee, first that I was wise, 545 (548)
Then temperate, and to thee greatly kind
And to my boys. Nay, patience, hear me out.
When I had come here from the Iolchian land,
Bringing with me a train of hindering cares,

What happier chance could I, an exile, find 550 (553)
Than this, to marry me with the king's child?
Not, thought which galls thee, sickened of thy bed
And wounded with desire for a new bride;
Nor striving for the crown of many sons—
For those I have suffice, I nought complain— 555 (558)
But, that which makes most, that we prosperous
Should dwell and not know scanting; well aware
That every friend will shun the poor man's path.—
Also that I might rear as fits my house
My children, and, giving brothers to thy sons,
Bind them in one, and having interknit 561 (564)
My family, live on in happy case.
For what needst thou more children? But to me
'Tis profit to advance my living sons 564 (566)
By those that shall be. Have I ill resolved?
Thyself, wert thou not galled about thy bed,
Couldst never say it. But to such a pass
You women are come now, that, your bed safe,
You think you have everything; but let ill luck
Touch that, and all that fairest is and best 570 (572)
You count most hateful. 'Twere a goodly boon
If men could raise their children otherwhence

And there should be no woman tribe at all;
So would there be no mischief in the world.

CHORUS.

Jason, these reasons hast thou tricked out well;
And yet, meseems, though I speak to thy distaste,
Thou dost not justly to betray thy wife.

MEDEA.

Sure many ways from many men I differ.
For him who does wrong and is wise to gloze it
'I hold worth worser doom. For making sure 580 (582)
He'll show wrong gracious with his tongue, he's bold
To every crime: yet he's not over wise —
As thou art not. Be no more specious with me
And cunning-phrased: one word o'ertopples thee;
It would have fitted thee, wert thou no knave, 585 (586)
To make this marriage with my won consent,
Instead of keeping secrecy from friends.

JASON.

Rarely wouldst thou have humoured the design,
Had I shown thee the marriage, thou too weak
Even now to put away thy heart's mad rage. 590 (590)

### Medea.
This moved thee not. But with a foreign wife
Thou hadst gone unexalted to old age.

### Jason.
Now this well know: not for the woman's sake
I wed me in this royal home, now mine,
But, as I said but now, having at heart  595 (595)
To keep thee safe and to thy sons to add
Sons kingly born, a safeguard to our house.

### Medea.
Never be mine a lordly bitter life,
Nor wealth which makes me agony of soul.

### Jason.
Go to, reverse thy prayer and show more wise. 600 (600)
Never let fortune's goods seem bitter to thee,
Nor deem thyself unhappy while thou thrivst.

### Medea.
Yes, flout me, since thou hast a refuge thine:
But I shall desolate depart this land.

### Jason.
Thyself didst choose it: blame not any else. 605 (605)

## Medea.
By what deeds? Marrying and forsaking thee?

## Jason.
Cursing impious curses on the royal house.

## Medea.
And I through thy house verily am cursed.

## Jason.
Tush! I'll no more dispute with thee of this.
But if thou for thy children and thyself   610 (610)
Wouldst, as a help in flight, take of my goods,
Speak, I am prompt to give with no churl's hand,
And to pledged guest-friends who will use thee well
Send tokens of old hospitalities.   614 (613)
And, woman, dost thou nay-say these, thou'rt mad:
But ceasing from thy rage thou'lt softlier fare.

## Medea.
Guest-friends of thine shall never profit me.
Nor will I aught of thee: proffer me nothing,
For there's no service in a bad man's gift.

## Jason.
Then do I call the gods to witness this,   620 (619)

How I desire to serve thee and thy sons,
Yet thou'lt not like good gifts but wantonly
Dost spurn thy friends, therefore shalt mourn the more.

### MEDEA.

Begone, for longing after thy new bride
Seizes thee so much tarrying from her home :  625 (624)
Take her, for it is like—yea, and possessed
By a god I will declare it—thou dost wed
With such a wedding as thou'lt wish undone.

### CHORUS.

#### STROPHE I.

The wild loves that force eager way
Nor worth nor fame on man confer,  630 (630)
But if come Cypris with meet sway
There is no gracious god like her.
  Oh never, queen, I pray,
Drive from thy golden bow into my heart
The escapeless passion-poisoned dart.  635 (634)

## CHORUS.

### Antistrophe I.

But be my guardian chastity,
The god's best gift, nor let my mind,
By cruel Cypris forced awry,
The burden of hot anger find,
    Of gnawing jealousy;        640 (639)
But may she, pleasured with calm wedded lives,
Wisely adjudge their lots to wives.

### Strophe II.

Oh home, oh country, ne'er may I
Through long hard years of poverty,
That bitterest of all distress,        645 (647)
Live on an alien citiless:
Nay, rather, having had my day,
Let death, let death do me away:
For no woe doth outpass this woe,
One's fatherland no more to know.    650 (652)

### Antistrophe II.

Yes, we ourselves have seen, our speech
Is not of words that others teach,
Since, by most dread despair brought low,
Thee hath no city cared for, no,
Nor any friend. Let shameful blight  6₅5 (658)
Slay him who gives not friends their right,
Unlocking them his heart's pure store:
Let him be friend of mine no more.

#### Ægeus.

Medea, hail; since sooth no fairer greeting 659 (663)
Hath any known wherewith to reverence friends.

#### Medea.

Oh hail, thou too, son of the wise Pandion,
Ægeus. Whence comst thou to this country's plains?

#### Ægeus.

Last from the ancient oracle of Phœbus.

#### Medea.

But wherefore sent to earth's prophetic centre?

#### Ægeus.

Searching how children might be raised to me. 665 (669)

MEDEA.

In heaven's name, leadst thou yet a childless life?

ÆGEUS.

Childless am I by some divine one's will.

MEDEA.

Hast thou a wife, or knowst no marriage-bed?

ÆGEUS.

I am not unharnessed to the marriage yoke.

MEDEA.

What then did Phœbus speak concerning sons?

ÆGEUS.

Words subtler than a man can puzzle out. 671 (675)

MEDEA.

Fits it I learn the sentence of the gods?

ÆGEUS.

Surely—the more that it needs crafty wit.

MEDEA.

What then declared he? Speak, if I may hear.

ÆGEUS.

I might not loose the wine-bag's jutting foot. 675 (679)

MEDEA.
Ere thou didst what or camst unto what land?

ÆGEUS.
Ere to my father's hearth I came again.

MEDEA.
Then seeking what to these shores didst thou sail?

ÆGEUS.
There is one Pittheus who is king of Trœzen.

MEDEA.
Of Pelops, so they say, most reverent son. 680 (684)

ÆGEUS.
To him would I impart the god's reply.

MEDEA.
For he is wise and in such matters versed.

ÆGEUS.
And brother in arms to me most dear of all.

MEDEA.
Now speed thee well, and gain what thou desirest.

ÆGEUS.
But thou, why is thine eye dulled and thy bloom?

MEDEA.

Ægeus, my husband is the chief of villains. 686 (690)

ÆGEUS.

What sayest thou? Speak me plainly all thy cares.

MEDEA.

Jason doth wrong me, nothing harmed by me.

ÆGEUS.

By what deed done? Tell me more certainly.

MEDEA.

Another wife is mistress of his home. 690 (694)

ÆGEUS.

What! hath he ventured this most shameless thing?

MEDEA.

Know it: I am dishonoured, I once dear.

ÆGEUS.

Whether fallen amorous or hating thee?

MEDEA.

Oh much enamoured! Faithless to old ties!

ÆGEUS.

Why, let him go being, as thou sayst, a villain.

MEDEA.

Of the king's alliance he fell amorous.  696 (700)

ÆGEUS.

Who gives the bride then? Go through with the tale.

MEDEA.

Creon, who governs this Corinthian realm.

ÆGEUS.

Sooth, lady, if thou weepest there's excuse.

MEDEA.

Undone! Aye, and from this land driven forth.

ÆGEUS.

By whom? Thou dost show yet another ill.  701 (705)

MEDEA.

Creon drives me from Corinthian ground an exile.

ÆGEUS.

Will Jason suffer it? I praise not this.

MEDEA.

Oh his words like it not; only he means
To bear it with a very valiant patience.  705 (708)
But thee, thee, I implore by this thy beard,
By these thy knees, and am thy suppliant,

Pity, pity me miserable wretch,
And never see me cast out desolate,
But take me to thy hearth in thy home and land.
So by the gods may thy desire of sons     711 (714)
Be brought to pass and mayst thou die content.
Aye, thou knowst not what find this thou hast found:
I'll stay thy childlessness, I'll have thee rear
A race of sons. Such philtres do I know. 715 (718)

### ÆGEUS.

For many reasons, lady, I am fain
This boon to give thee: for the gods' sake first:
Next for those sons whose birth thou dost assure;
For until now I am without all hope.
But 'tis thus with me : if indeed thou comst
Into my realm I will endeavour thee     721 (724)
Such host's protection as a just man may:
But this much, lady, I forewarn thee well,
I will not lead thee with me from this land;
Yet, if thyself thou comst into my house,     725 (727)
Thou shalt dwell sheltered and to none I'll yield thee.
Now from this soil thyself withdraw thy foot:
Both to my hosts and thee I would be leal.

MEDEA.

It shall be thus. But, were an oath of this
Accorded me, all done by thee were gracious.

ÆGEUS.

Dost thou not trust me? What disturbs thy faith?

MEDEA.

I trust thee, but the house of Pelias
Now, is mine enemy, and Creon too.
Surely to these thou wouldst not, yoked by oaths,
Yield me if they would hale me from thy land:
But only bound by words, not sworn to the gods,
Thou mightest become their friend, mayhap be won
By herald-proffers: because I am weak,
But theirs are riches and a royal home.  739 (740)

ÆGEUS.

Much foresight hast thou spoken, lady. Now,
If it likes thee this should be, I gainsay not:
And unto me too were it the more safe
To have excuse to shew thine enemies,
And thou wert surer fenced. Name thou what gods.

MEDEA.

Swear by the plains of Earth and by the Sun, 745 (746).
My father's father—add the gods' whole race.

ÆGEUS.

To do what deed or what to do not? Speak.

MEDEA.

Neither thyself ever to drive me forth
Out of thy land, nor, if some foe would take me,
To yield me in thy life of thy consent.   750 (751)

ÆGEUS.

By Earth I swear, and the splendour of the Sun,
And all the gods, to stand by what thou sayst.

MEDEA.

Enough. But, breaking faith, what curse on thee?

ÆGEUS.

Such as do use to fall on impious men.

MEDEA.

Depart in peace, for all is well: but I   755 (756)
With utmost speed will to thy realm repair,
Having ended that I do, gained that I long for.

· CHORUS.

Now Maia's son, the wayfarer's lord,
  Bring thee to thy home:
And that next thy heart, which thou eagerest for,
Mayst thou attain; for a noble man,
  Ægeus, thou seemst unto me.

MEDEA.

Oh Zeus, and Right the child of Zeus, and thou
Light of the Sun! Now, now, friends, shall be mine
A goodly victory on mine enemies,    765 (765)
And I do tread the path: now is there hope
Mine enemies shall pay the penalty.
For this man, when I was in greatest stress,
Reveals himself a harbour for my schemes:
To whom my mooring tackle will I fix,    770 (770)
Having reached the town and citadel of Pallas.
And now to thee I'll speak all my resolves:
Hearken then words tuned to no pleasant mirth.
Sending one of my household I'll intreat
That Jason come into my sight: he come,    775 (775)
I'll speak him meek sweet words—as that his doings
Seem goodly to me and become him well;

Then I'll implore him that my sons may stay—
Not in an unkind land to leave my children
To the despitings of mine enemies,   780 (782)
But to destroy the king's child by my wiles:
For I will send them, holding gifts in hand,
To bear the bride, that they be not driven hence,
And if she take the gauds and prank her in them
She shall die horribly, and with her too   785 (788)
Whoso shall touch the girl: with such rare salves
Will I anoint the gifts.  Thus then I end
That theme.  But I am woe for what a deed
Needs must be done: for I shall slay my sons.
No one there is who may deliver them.   790 (793)
And, having hurled down the whole house of Jason,
I shall go forth this land, flying the curse
Of my dear children's death and having borne
To do the most unhallowed of all deeds.
For, oh my friends, the mockeries of foes   795 (797)
May not be borne.  Well, be it as it must be.
What good for me to live?  No home for me,
Nor fatherland, nor refuge from my woes.
Oh then I erred when I went forth and left
My father's house lured by a Hellene's talk,   800 (801)

Who, with the god's help, shall pay forfeit yet.
For neither shall he more behold alive
His sons by me nor shall his new made wife
Bear to him other sons, since the ill wench
Shall die an ill death, doomed by my drugged salves.
Let none believe me weak and lethargic     806 (807)
Nor tame in spirit, but far other souled;
Dour to my foes, but to my friends most helpful:
For the lives of such do wear the nobler grace.

#### CHORUS.

Now, since thou hast possessed us of thy thought,
Much anxious both to serve thee and give help
To human laws, I urge thee, do not thus. 812 (813)

#### MEDEA.

It may no otherwise. But 'tis excused
That thou so speak'st, who bear'st not wrongs as I.

#### CHORUS.

But, lady, hast thou heart to kill thy sons?     815 (816)

#### MEDEA.

Since thus my husband's heart were deepest stung.

CHORUS.

But thou wert then the woefullest of women.

MEDEA.

So be it. Wasted are all tempering words.
(*To the Nurse*)
But thou, go, speed thee and bring Jason here;
For I do use thee in all trusty things.  820 (821)
But nothing speak of that I have resolved
If thou mean thy mistress well and be true woman.


CHORUS.

STROPHE I.

The Athenians, great from long ago,
And children of the gods in heaven,
Still for their daily nurture know  825 (827)
The loftiest food of wisdom given
A hallowed and unconquered state;
And, through their bright translucent air,
Move ever with proud jubilant gait,
　　There, as old rhymes relate,  830 (831)
Where erst Harmonia, of the yellow hair,
The virgin nine Pierian muses bare.

## Antistrophe I.

There too, the ancient lay runs thus,
Once Cypris, quaffing from the wave
Of crystal flowing Cephissus,            835 (835)
O'er all the land her soft breath drave
In tender wafts of scented wind:
And, donning ever her sweet crown
Of rose-bloom in her loose locks twined,
    Her vassal loves, assigned           840 (844)
Kind ministers to wisdom, she sends down,
And helpmates in all deeds of good renown.


## Strophe II.

    The land of sacred waters, then,
    The city of good will to men,
    How shall it have a welcoming      845 (849)
    For thee, a too unholy thing
    To dwell with others, murderess thou
    Of thine own children? Oh, take heed;
    Think, think on thy sons' death-blow now;
    Think, think upon thy deadly deed.    850 (852)

Nay, by thy knees, by every prayer,
We all invoke thee, oh forbear:
Thou shalt not slay thy sons: forbear.

### Antistrophe II.

And how then couldst thou ever find
Force in thy hand, thy heart, thy mind, 855 (856)
Against thy sons, thine own, to wreak
The dreadful vengeance thou dost seek?
And how, if but a moment long
Upon thy sons thy glance should wait,
Wilt thou indeed continue strong 860 (861)
And tearless to fulfil their fate?
It is not thine, not possibly,
When at thy feet the children cry
In their life-blood thy fell hand to dye.

### Jason.

Summoned, I come. For, though thou'rt rancourous, 865 (866)
Thou shalt not fail of this, but I will hear,
Lady, what new boon thou wouldst have of me.

MEDEA.

Jason, I pray thee, be to my past words
Forgiving. For thou shouldst bear with my passion,
Since once there was much love between us two.
But I have taken counsel with myself     871 (872)
And chid me: "Oh cross fool, why do I rave,
And am in wrath at those who plan me good?
And why stand I at war with this realm's lords
And with my husband who, in that he does,     875 (876)
Does it for our most profit, marrying him
A royal bride and giving my sons brothers?
Shall I not turn from anger? What my hurt,
For whom the gods so graciously provide?
Truly have I not children, and do know     880 (880)
We are but fugitives and poor of friends?"
And, having pondered these things, I discerned
My much unreason and how fond my rage.
Now therefore I approve, and politic
Account thee taking to us this alliance,     885 (885)
But myself witless, I who should have shared
Thy counsels with thee and accomplished them,
Stood by the bed and joyed to tend the bride.
But what we are we are—I'll say no worse—

Women. Then fits not thou shouldst even thee
To baseness nor with folly answer folly.  891 (891)
I do submit and say I then judged ill,
But now I wiselier have resolved of this.
Boys, boys, come hither, quit the house, approach,
Greet ye your father, speak to him with me,  895 (895)
And from the former hatred be now changed,
Together with your mother, into friends.
For we've made covenant, and laid by wrath.
Take his right hand—Ah me! the woeful day!—
Lo what unshaped forebodings vex my soul!  900 (900)
Why, children, ye will thus, in a long life
Stretch forth your dear arms to him? Oh poor me,
How prone to weep am I and full of dread.
But, freeing me of quarrel with your father,
My trembling sight has filled itself with tears. 905 (905)

CHORUS.

In mine eyes too the dewy tear hath sprung—
And may the present ill not pass to worse.

JASON.

Lady, these words I praise, nor blame the former;
For 'tis of woman's kind against a spouse

Trafficking in new marriages to rage. 910 (910)
Now to the better part thine heart has turned,
And thou, though late, dost own the mastering will.
Conduct of a wise woman, this. For you,
My boys, your father, not uncarefully,
Has spent much forethought with the gods' good
    help, 915 (915)
Since you, I trow, shall with your brothers yet
Be first in Corinth's land. But grow and thrive:
The rest your father or what god is kind
Will bring about. And may I see you bloom
Waxed to youth's prime, triumphant on my foes.
Thou why with new tears dost thou dew thine eyes,
Turning thy wan cheek from me, nor dost greet
With any gladness yet these words of mine?

### MEDEA.

'Tis nothing. I am troubled for my sons.

### JASON.

Be of good courage: I will care for them. 925 (926)

### MEDEA.

I will. Surely I shall not doubt thy word.
But woman's a poor she thing and born to cry.

### Jason.
Why, prithee, for the boys make such laments?

### Medea.
I gave them birth: and when thou didst speak hopes
The boys should live, a qualm came over me   930 (931)
Whether it should go thus. Well, but why now
Thou hast this talk with me is told in part;
Of the rest I will make mention. Since it hath pleased
The royal house to send me from the land,
For me too it is best, I know it well,   935 (935)
Not to dwell here, a thwarting thing to thee
And to the country's sovereigns. For I seem
As though I had a quarrel to their house.
But verily we'll hasten from this land.   939 (938)
And yet, that thine own hand may train the boys,
Pray Creon that they shall not leave his realm.

### Jason.
It must be tried. With what success I know not.

### Medea.
Why then, bid thou thy wife entreat her father
To the end the children shall not leave his realm.

JASON.

Certes.  I look too to prevail with her,  945 (944)
If she be such as other women are.

MEDEA.

I too will share with thee in the attempt,
For I will send her gifts more beautiful
By far than are among men now, I know :  949 (948)
A fine-webbed robe and garland of wrought gold :
My sons shall bear them.  Now then with all haste
Let some one of my servants bring the gauds.
She shall be rich, not in one thing but many,
Gaining thee a perfect husband to her spouse,
And having hers the gauds which erst the Sun,
My father's father, gave those born from him. 956 (955)
Boys, take this wedding dower into your hands,
Carry them to the happy royal bride :
Give them—she will not have unworthy gifts.

JASON.

Yet why, fond fool, lose these out of thy keep?  960 (959)
Dost think the kingly house is scant of robes?
Or gold, dost think?  Preserve these, give them not :

For, if my wife set any store on me,
I well know she will prize me over bribes.

### MEDEA.

Thwart me not. Gifts, they say, win even gods,
And gold makes more with men than countless reasons.
Fate sides with her; the god exalts her now;
She queens it young. But I, not with mere gold,
With my own life, would buy my sons from exile.
Come, children, go now to her lordly home,   970 (969)
Go to your father's new wife and my mistress,
Pray her, beseech, that ye leave not this realm,
Offering the gauds: for chiefly it behoves
That she receive our gifts in her own hands.
Go with all haste. And may you to your mother
Become glad messengers of that she hopes.   976 (975)

### CHORUS.

#### Strophe I.

No hope left us now for the children's life;
No hope; they are passing on to death;
And the gift that comes to the new-made wife
Is the gift of a curse in her golden wreath.   980 (979)

Alas for her doom!
Round about her yellow hair
Her own hand will set it there,
Signet jewel of the tomb.

### Antistrophe I.

By the grace and the perfect gleaming won   985 (982)
She will place the gold-wrought crown on her head,
She will robe herself in the robe; and anon
She will deck her a bride among the dead.
    Alas for her doom!
    Fallen in such snare, too late   990 (989)
    Would she struggle from her fate,
    Hers the death-lot of the tomb.

### Strophe II.

But thou, oh wretched man, oh woeful-wed,
Yet marriage-linked to kings; thou all unseeing,
    Who nearest fast   995 (993)
A swift destruction to thy children's being,
A hateful death to her who shares thy bed,
Oh hapless man, how fallen from thy past!

### Antistrophe II.

And miserable mother of fair boys,
We mourn too thy despair with outburst weeping,
    Thine who wouldst kill     1001 (996)
Thy sons for the wife's couch where lonely sleeping
Thy husband leaves thee for new lawless joys
With a new homemate who thy place shall fill.

### Attendant.

Mistress, thy children are forgiven from exile: 1005 (1002)
And in her hands the queenly bride, well pleased,
Received the gifts. Thence goodwill to thy sons.

### Medea.

Alas!

### Attendant.

Why dost thou stand aghast when thou hast prospered?

### Medea.

Woe's me!

### Attendant.

This chimes not with the tidings I declare.

### Medea.

Woe's me again.

ATTENDANT.
I have not heralded mischance I know not, 1010 (1009)
And missed my joy of bringing happy news?

MEDEA.
Thou hast brought what thou hast brought: I blame
thee not.

ATTENDANT.
Why then dost droop thine eyes and dost weep tears?

MEDEA.
There is much cause, old man. For this the gods
And I by my own wild resolves have wrought. 1015 (1014)

ATTENDANT.
Take heart. For through thy sons thou'lt yet return.

MEDEA.
Alas, I shall send others home ere that.

ATTENDANT.
Thou'rt not the only one torn from her sons,
And being mortal lightly shouldst bear griefs.

MEDEA.
And so I will. But go thou in the house, 1020 (1019)
Prepare my children what the day requires.

Oh sons, my sons, for you there is a home
And city where, forsaking wretched me,
Ye shall still dwell and have no mother more:
But I, an exile, seek another land,     1025 (1024)
Ere I have joyed in you and seen you glad,
Ere I have decked for you the nuptial pomp,
The bride, the bed, and held the torch aloft.
Oh me! forlorn by my untempered moods!
In vain then have I nurtured ye, my sons,   1030 (1029)
In vain have toiled and been worn down by cares,
And felt the hard child-bearing agonies.
There was a time when I, unhappy one,
Had many hopes in you, that both of you
Would cherish me in age and that your hands,
When I am dead, would fitly lay me out—   1036 (1034)
That wish of all men: but now lost indeed
Is that sweet thought, for I must, reft of you,
Live on a piteous life and full of pain:
And ye, your dear eyes will no more behold   1040 (1038)
Your mother, gone into your new strange life.
Alas! Why do ye fix your eyes on me,
My sons? Why smile ye on me that last smile?
Alas! What must I do? For my heart faints,

Thus looking on my children's happy eyes. 1045 (1043)
Women, I cannot. Farewell my past resolves.
My boys go forth with me. What boots it me
To wring their father with their cruel fates,
And earn myself a doubled misery?
It shall not be, shall not. Farewell resolves. 1050 (1048)
And yet what mood is this? Am I content
To spare my foes and be a laughing-stock?
It must be dared. Why, out upon my weakness
To let such coward thoughts steal from my heart!
Go, children, to the house. And he who lacks
Right now to stand by sacrifice of mine, 1056 (1054)
Let him look to it. I'll not stay my hand.
    Alas! alas!
No surely. Oh my heart thou canst not do it;
Racked heart, let them go safely, spare the boys:
Living far hence with me they'll make thee joy.
No; by the avenging demon-gods in hell, 1061 (1059)
Never shall be that I should yield my boys
To the despitings of mine enemies.
For all ways they must die, and, since 'tis so,
Better I slay them, I who gave them birth. 1065 (1063)
All ways 'tis fated: there is no escape.

5—2

For now, in the robes, the wealth upon her head,
The royal bride is perishing; I know it.
But, since I go on so forlorn a journey
And them too send on one yet more forlorn,  1070 (1068)
I'd fain speak with my sons. Give me, my children,
Give your mother your right hands to clasp to her.
Oh darling hands, oh dearest lips to me,
Oh forms and noble faces of my boys!
Be happy: but *there*. For of all part here  1075 (1073)
'Your father has bereft you. Oh sweet kiss,
Oh grateful breath and soft skin of my boys!
Go, go. I can no longer look on you,
But by my sufferings am overborne.
Oh I do know what sorrows I shall make,  1080 (1078)
But anger keeps the mastery of my thoughts,
Which is the chiefest cause of human woes.

CHORUS.

Oftentimes now have I ere to-day
Reached subtler reasons, joined higher debates,
Than womanhood has the right to scan.  1085 (1084)
But 'tis that with us too there walks a muse
Discoursing high things—yet not to us all,

Since few of the race of women there be,
(Thou wert like to find among many but one),
    Not friendless of any muse.     1090 (1089)
And now I aver that of mortals those
Who have never wed, or known children theirs,
    Than parents are happier far.
For the childless at least, through not making essay
If sons be born for a joy or a curse,     1095 (1095)
Having none are safe from much miseries.
But such as have springing up in their homes
Sweet blossom and growth of children, them
I see worn with cares through the weary while:
First how to rear them in seemly wise   (1100) (1101)
And how to leave the children estate;
Then next, whether they are spending themselves
For ignoble beings or for good,
    That is left dark from their ken.
But one last ill of all to all men     1105 (1105)
Now will I speak. For if they have found
Sufficing estate, and their children have waxed
To the glory of youth, and moreover are good,
If their lot have chanced to them thus, lo Death,
Vanished back to his Hades again,     1110 (1110)

Has snatched the forms of the children away.
And what avails it for children's sake
To have the gods heap on mortals' heads
    This bitterest deadly despair?

###### MEDEA.

Friends, now for long abiding the event,   1115 (1116)
Eager I gaze for what shall come of it;
And now discern a servitor of Jason's
Advancing hither. And his gasping breath
Declares him messenger of some dire news.

###### MESSENGER.

Oh thou who hast wrought a horrible wild deed,
Medea, fly, fly, sparing not car of the waves   1121 (1122)
Nor chariot hurrying thee across the plains.

###### MEDEA.

But what hath chanced to me worth such a flight?

###### MESSENGER.

The royal maiden is this moment dead,   1124 (1125)
With Creon her father, by thy magic drugs.

###### MEDEA.

Thou hast told sweetest news. From henceforth rank
Among my benefactors and my friends.

##### MESSENGER.

What sayst thou? Lady, hast thou thy right wits,
Nor ravst, who, having outraged the king's hearth,
Joyst at the hearing and dost nothing fear? 1130 (1131)

##### MEDEA.

Somewhat in sooth I have to answer back
To these thy words. But be not hasty, friend.
Come, tell me how they died. For twice so much
Wilt thou delight me if they died in torments.

##### MESSENGER.

When then the boys, thy two sons, had arrived,
And with their father entered the bride's house,
We servants, who were troubled for thy griefs,
Rejoiced: and much talk shortly filled our ears,
Thou and thy husband had made up past strife.
One kissed the hand and one the golden head
Of thy young sons, and I myself, for joy, 1141 (1142)
Followed the boys into the women's halls.
But our mistress, whom we serve now in thy place,
Before she saw thy sons come side by side
Kept her glad gaze on Jason: then ere long 1145 (1146)
She hid her eyes and turned away from him

Her whitened face, loathing the boys' approach.
But thy husband checked his young bride's heat and
    rage, 1148 (1150)
Thus speaking, " Be not rancorous to thy friends,
But cease thy wrath and turn again thy head,
Counting those dear who're to thy husband dear.
Take then their gifts, and of thy father pray
He spare for my sake my boys' banishment."
And when she saw the gauds she said no nay,
But spoke her husband sooth in all.  And ere
The father and the boys had gone far forth 1156 (1158)
She took the shimmering robes and put them on,
And, setting round her curls the golden crown,
At the bright mirror stroked her tresses right,
And smiled on the mute likeness of herself. 1160 (1162)
Next, risen from her couch, flits through the room,
Daintily tripping on her milk-white feet,
With the gifts overjoyed, often and long
O'er her slant shoulder gazing on herself.
But then a sight came dread to look upon; 1165 (1167)
For, a change come on her hue, she staggers back,
Shuddering in every limb, and scarce wins time
To fall upon her couch, not to the ground.

Then an old waiting dame, who deemed the wrath
Of Pan or other god had come on her,  1170 (1172)
Shrilled the prayer-chaunt; I trow before she saw
The white foam oozing through the mouth, the eyes
Start from their sockets strained, the bloodless flesh.
For then, far other wailing than her chaunt, 1174 (1176)
Came her great shriek. Straight, to the father's house
Rushed one, another to the new-wed husband,
To tell of the bride's fate; and all the house
Was ringing with incessant hurrying steps.  1178 (1180)
By this might a swift walker stretching limb
Have touched the goal of the six plethra course,
And she, who had been speechless, with shut eyes,
Fearfully moaned, poor wretch, and started up:
For twofold anguish did make war on her. 1183 (1185)
For both the golden crown set round her head
Was sending marvellous streams of eating fire,
And the fine-webbed robe, the offering of thy sons,
Was gnawing at the hapless one's white flesh.
But she, sprung from her couch, now flies, ablaze,
Tossing her head and curls this way and that,
Fain to dash off the crown. But all too firm
The golden headband clave; and still the fire

Flamed doubly fiercer when she tossed her locks.
And, conquered by her fate, she drops to the floor;
Scarce, but by her own father to be known:
For neither the grave sweetness of her eyes  1195 (1197)
Nor her fair face was visible; but blood
Mingled with flame was welling from her head,
And, by the secret poison gnawed, her flesh
Dropped from the bones, as resin-gouts from the fir—
Dreadful to see.  And none dared touch the dead.
For her fate had we to our monitor.  1201 (1203)
But the hapless father, through his ignorance
Of how she perished, having ere we knew
Entered the chamber, falls upon the corse,
Breaks instant into wailing, and, her body  1205 (1206)
Enfolded in his clasp, he kisses her
Thus calling on her, "Oh unhappy child,
What god hath foully done thee thus to death?
Who makes this charnel heap of mouldering age
Thy childless mourner? Oh woe worth the while!
Would now that I might die with thee, my child."
But, when he stayed his sobbings and laments
And would have raised his aged body up,
He, as the ivy by the laurel's boughs,

By the fine-webbed robes was caught; and fearful
  grew                                           1215 (1214)
The struggle.  He sought on his knees to rise:
She held him back.  And if by force he rose
He tore the aged flesh from off his bones.
And then at length the evil-fated man    1219 (1218)
Ceased and gave up the ghost, able no more
To cope with that great anguish.  And they lie,
Father and daughter, corpses side by side:
A sight of sorrow that appeals for tears.
And truly let thy fortunes be apart
From reasonings of mine: for thou thyself  1225 (1223)
Wilt know a shelter from the retribution.
But not now first I count the lot of man
A passing shadow: and I might say those
Of mortals who are very seeming wise     1229 (1225)
And fret themselves with learnings, those are they
Who make them guilty of the chiefest folly;
But no one mortal is a happy man,
Though, riches flooding in, more prosperous
One than another grow; yet none is happy.

CHORUS.

Fortune, it seems, on Jason will to-day   1235 (1231)
Justly heap many woes.  Oh hapless one,
Daughter of Creon, how we mourn thy fate,
Who to the halls of Hades art gone forth
Because of Jason's marrying with thee.

MEDEA.

My friends, this purpose stand approved to me,
Slaying my boys to hurry from this realm;   1241 (1237)
Not, making weak delays, to give my sons
By other and more cruel hands to die.
Nay, steel thyself my heart.  Why linger we
As not to do that horror which yet *must* be?   1245 (1243)
Come, oh my woeful hand, take take the sword:
On to my new life's mournful starting point,
And be no coward, nor think on thy boys,
How dear, how thou didst give them birth.  Nay rather
For this short day forget they are thy sons:   1250 (1248)
Then weep them afterwards.  For though thou slay'st them
Oh but they're dear, and I a desolate woman.

## CHORUS.

### Strophe.

Earth, and all-lighting glow of Sun,
    Behold, behold;
See this sad woman and undone,     1255 (1253)
Ere yet her murderous hand, made bold
Against her own, her children slay.
For they sprang of the golden stem
Of thy descent; and great to-day
Our dread the blood of gods in them     1260 (1256)
Shall by a mortal's wrath be spilt.
But now do thou, oh Zeus-born light,
Stay her, prevent; put thou to flight
That fell Erinnys to this home
From gods avenging past crimes come     1265 (1259)
To whelm her in despair and guilt.

### Antistrophe.

Upon thy children has thy care
    Been spent in vain;
In vain thy loved babes didst thou bear;
Thou who the inhospitable lane     1270 (1263)

Of the dark rocks Symplegades
Didst leave behind thee in thy wake.
Forlorn one, why do pangs like these
Of passion thy torn spirit shake?
Why shall stern murder of them grow?　1275 (1267)
For scarce is any cleansing found
Of kindred blood that from the ground
For vengeance cries: but like for like
The gods send curses down and strike
The slayers and their houses low.　1280 (1270)

### First Son.

Alas!
What shall I do? Whither run from our mother?

### Second Son.

I know not, dearest brother, for we perish.

### Chorus.

Dost hear thy children, hear their cry of pain?
　Oh luckless woman, desperate!
Shall I within the house then? I were fain　1285 (1275)
　To shield the children from such fate.

### First Son.

Ho! in the gods' name, rescue! There is need.

### Second Son.

For we are in the toils, beneath the knife.

### Chorus.

Oh cruel, what, of stone or steel art thou,
    Thou who that bloom         1290 (1279)
Of sons thyself didst bear wouldst see die now
    By thine hands' doom?
One woman have I heard of, one alone
And of the far-off days, whose deathful hand
Was laid upon the babes that were her own,   1295 (1283)
Ino by gods distraught when from her land
She by the queenly spouse of Zeus was banned,
    Sent to roam to and fro;
And, seeking her sons' death, she, wild with woe,
Stretched forth her foot from off the sea's rough
    strand,                       1300 (1287)
Whelmed her with them into the waves below,
    And, they so dying with her, died.
Henceforth can aught called strange or dread betide?

Oh bed of woman, with all mischief fraught,
What ills hast thou ere now to mortals brought!

### JASON.

Women, ye who thus stand about the house,  1306 (1293)
Is she within her home who wrought these crimes,
Medea, or hath she gone away in flight?
For now must she or hide beneath the earth
Or lift herself with wings into wide air   1310 (1297)
Not to pay forfeit to the royal house.
Thinks she, having slain the rulers of this land,
Herself uninjured from this home to fly?
But not of her I reck as of my sons:
Her those she wronged will evilly requite,   1315 (1302)
But to preserve my children's life I came,
Lest to my hurt the avenging kin on them
Wreak somewhat for their mother's bloody crime.

### CHORUS.

Oh wretched man! What woes thou comst to, Jason,
Thou knowst not, else hadst thou not said these words.

### JASON.

What is it? Seeks she then to kill me too?  1321 (1308)

CHORUS.

The boys have perished by their mother's hand.

JASON.

Woe! What sayst thou? Woman, how thou destroyst me!

CHORUS.

As now no more in being count thy sons.

JASON.

Where killed she them, in the house or without?

CHORUS.

Open these gates, thou'lt see thy murdered sons.

JASON.

Undo the bolt on the instant, servants there, 1327 (1314)
Loose the clamps, that I may see my grief and bane,
May see them dead and guerdon her with death.

MEDEA (*from overhead*).

Why dost thou batter at these gates, and force them,
Seeking the dead and me who wrought their deaths?
Cease from this toil. If thou hast need of me 1332 (1319)
Speak then, if thou wouldst aught. But never more
Thy hand shall touch me; such a chariot

The Sun, my father's father, gives to me,  1335 (1321)
A stronghold from the hand of enemies.


JASON.

Oh loathsome thing, oh woman most abhorred
Of gods and me and all the race of men,
Thou who hast dared to thrust the sword in thy sons
Thyself didst bear, and hast destroyed me out,
Childless.  And thou beholdest sun and earth,
Who didst this, daredst this most accursed deed!
Perish.  Oh, I am wise now, then unwise,
When from thy home in thy barbarian land
I brought thee with me to a Hellene house,  1345 (1331)
A monstrous bane; to the land that nurtured thee
And to thy father traitress.  Now at me
Have the gods launched thy retributory fiends,
Who, slaying first thy brother at the hearth,
Hiedst thee unto the stately-prowed ship Argo.
Such thy first deeds: then, married to myself  1351 (1336)
And having borne me children, for a spite
Of beddings and weddings thou hast slaughtered them.
There's not a Hellene woman had so dared;
Above whom I, forsooth, choose thee to wife—

A now loathed tie and ruinous to me— 1356 (1341)
Thee lioness not woman, of a mood
Than the Tursenian Scylla more untamed.
Enough; for not with thousands of rebukes
Could I wring thee, such is thine hardihood. 1360 (1345)
Avaunt, thou guilty shame! child-murderess!
But mine it is to wail my present fate;
Who nor of my new spousals shall have gain,
Nor shall have sons whom I begot and bred,
To call my living own: for I have lost them. 1365 (1350)

MEDEA.

I would have largely answered back thy words
If Zeus the father knew not what from me
Thou didst receive and in what kind hast done.
And 'twas not for thee, having spurned my love,
To lead a merry life, flouting at me, 1370 (1355)
Nor for the princess; neither was it his
Who gave her thee to wed, Creon, unscathed,
To cast me out of this his realm. And now,
If it is so like thee, call me lioness
And Scylla, dweller on Tursenian plains, 1375 (1359)
For as right bade me I have clutched thy heart.

JASON.

And thou too sufferest, partner in the pangs.

MEDEA.

True, but the pain profits if thou shalt not flout.

JASON.

Oh sons, how foul a mother have ye had!

MEDEA.

Oh boys, how died ye by your father's guilt! 1380 (1364)

JASON.

Not this right hand of mine slew them, indeed.

MEDEA.

No, but thine outrage and new wedding ties.

JASON.

So for a bed lost thou thoughtst fit to slay them?

MEDEA.

Dost thou count that a light wrong to a woman?

JASON.

Aye, to a chaste one: but thou'rt wholly base. 1385 (1369)

MEDEA.

They are no more. For this will torture thee.

JASON.

They are, I say—a haunting curse for thee.

MEDEA.

Who first begun the wrong the gods do know.

JASON.

Thy loathly mind they verily do know.

MEDEA.

Thou'rt hateful: and I'm sick of thy cross talk.

JASON.

And I of thine: but the farewell is easy.   1391 (1375)

MEDEA.

Well, how? What shall I do? I too long for it.

JASON.

Let me then bury and bemoan these dead. ✓

MEDEA.

Never. Since I will bury them with this hand,
Bearing them to the sacred grove of Hera,   1395 (1379)
God of the heights, that no one of my foes
Shall do despite to them, breaking their graves.
And I'll appoint this land of Sisyphus
A solemn high day and a sacrifice

For aye, because of their unhallowed deaths.
But I go to the city of Erechtheus,    1401 (1384)
To dwell with Ægeus there, Pandion's son.
For thee, as is most fit, thou, an ill man,
Shalt die an ill death, thy head battered in
By the ruins of thine Argo: that, to thee,   1405 (1387)
The sharp last sequel of our wedding tie.

### JASON.

But thee may thy children's Erinnys slay
  And Vengeance for blood.

### MEDEA.

And who among gods and friends will hear thee,
Betrayer of strangers and breaker of oaths?   1410 (1392)

### JASON.

Out, out, stained wretch and child murderess.

### MEDEA.

Go now to thy home and bury thy bride.

### JASON.

I go. Yea, of both my children bereft.

### MEDEA.

Thy wail is yet nothing. Wait and grow old.

JASON.

Oh, sons, much loved!

MEDEA.

Of their mother not thee. 1415 (1397)

JASON.

And yet thou didst slay them.

MEDEA.

Making thee woe.

JASON.

Alas! alas! I, a woeful man,
Desire to kiss the dear lips of my boys.

MEDEA.

Thou callst on them now, hast welcomes now;
Then didst reject them.

JASON.

In the gods' name, 1420 (1402)
Give me to touch my children's soft flesh.

MEDEA.

It may not be: thy words are vain waste.

JASON.

Oh Zeus, dost thou hear how I'm kept at bay,

And this that is done unto me of her,
This foul and child-slaying lioness?  1425 (1407)
But still to my utmost as best I may
I make these death-wails and invokings for them;
Thus to my witness calling the gods,
How thou, having slain my sons, dost prevent
That I touch with my hand and bury the dead—
Whom would I had never begotten so  1431 (1413)
By thee to behold them destroyed.

CHORUS.

Zeus in Olympus parts out many lots,
And the gods work to many undreamed of ends,
And that we looked for is never fulfilled,  1435 (1417)
And to things not looked for the gods make a way :
Even so hath this issue been.

# PASSAGES

in which the text taken departs from that of Paley.

Lines 40, 41 (39, 42).
Between these lines Paley retains the distich which recurs at
l. 380, 381 (379, 380).

Line 41 (42).
Τυράννους (Hermann).  For τύραννον (Paley).

Lines 132, 133 (133).
Κολχίδος· οὐδέ πω ἤπιος; (Porson).  For Κολχίδος, οὐδέ πω
ἤπιος· (Paley).

Line 134 (134).
'Απ' ἀμφιπύλου (Paley's conjecture).  For ἐπ' ἀμφιπύλου
(which he keeps in his text).

Lines 582, 583 (583, 584).
Ἔστι δ' οὐκ ἄγαν σοφός, ὡς καὶ σύ· μὴ νῦν κ.τ.λ.  (Witzschel).
For ἔστι δ' οὐκ ἄγαν σοφός. ὡς καὶ σὺ μὴ νῦν κ.τ.λ.  (Paley).

### Line 705 (708).

Καρτερεῖν δὲ βούλεται (the common reading). For καρτερεῖν δ' οὐ βούλεται (Paley).

### Line 736 (737).

Ἀνώμοτος (Porson, Dindorf, Elmsley). For ἐνώμοτος (Paley).

### Lines 783, 784 (785, 787).

Between these two lines Paley inserts a line which Elmsley leaves out as recurring at l. 950 (949).

### Lines 1064, 1065 (1062, 1063).

These lines which recur between l. 1243, 1244 (1239, 1242), are omitted in the latter place. Paley thinks they should be retained there and omitted here.

*Works by Augusta Webster.*

THE PROMETHEUS BOUND OF ÆSCHYLUS.
Literally translated into English Verse. Extra fcap. 8vo. 3s. 6d.

DRAMATIC STUDIES. Extra fcap. 8vo. 5s.

A WOMAN SOLD, and other Poems. Extra fcap. 8vo. 7s. 6d.

MACMILLAN AND CO: LONDON AND CAMBRIDGE.

www.ingramcontent.com/pod-product-compliance
Lightning Source LLC
Chambersburg PA
CBHW020302090426
42735CB00009B/1185